The Quigleys Have Got Talent

☆ ☆ ☆ ☆ ☆

Written by Simon Mason
Illustrated by Claire Clements

Published by Pearson Education Limited, Edinburgh Gate, Harlow, Essex, CM20 2JE
Registered company number: 872828

www.pearsonschools.co.uk

Text © Simon Mason 2011

Designed by Bigtop

Original illustrations © Pearson Education 2011

Illustrated by Claire Clements

The right of Simon Mason to be identified as author of this work has been asserted by him in accordance with the Copyright, Designs and Patents Act 1988.

First published 2011

15 14
10 9 8 7 6 5 4

British Library Cataloguing in Publication Data
A catalogue record for this book is available from the British Library

ISBN 978 1 408 27385 2

Copyright notice
All rights reserved. No part of this publication may be reproduced in any form or by any means (including photocopying or storing it in any medium by electronic means and whether or not transiently or incidentally to some other use of this publication) without the written permission of the copyright owner, except in accordance with the provisions of the Copyright, Designs and Patents Act 1988 or under the terms of a licence issued by the Copyright Licensing Agency, Saffron House, 6–10 Kirby Street, London ECIN 8TS (www.cla.co.uk). Applications for the copyright owner's written permission should be addressed to the publisher.

Printed and bound in Malaysia (CTP-VVP)

Acknowledgements
We would like to thank the children and teachers of Bangor Central Integrated Primary School, NI; Bishop Henderson C of E Primary School, Somerset; Brookside Community Primary School, Somerset; Cheddington Combined School, Buckinghamshire; Cofton Primary School, Birmingham; Dair House Independent School, Buckinghamshire; Deal Parochial School, Kent; Newbold Riverside Primary School, Rugby and Windmill Primary School, Oxford for their invaluable help in the development and trialling of the Bug Club resources.

Every effort has been made to contact copyright holders of material reproduced in this book. Any omissions will be rectified in subsequent printings if notice is given to the publishers.

Contents

Never Together   5

Magic Uncle Joe   14

The Great Quiglondo   21

Joint Winners   39

HAVE YOU GOT TALENT?

We're looking for the best act of the year!

Pick up your entry form from:

Mr Sheringham
Room 5

Never Together

Will Quigley was tall and excitable. His sister Lucy was small and determined. In spite of this, they went to the same school.

One day at school a poster went up. There was going to be a talent show. All acts were welcome, and the top prize was a VIP trip to a television studio and a large amount of spending money.

Will hurried off to find his friend Tim. For several months they had been learning judo together and had already mastered a range of throws, chokes and strangleholds. Will thought that a demonstration bout, perhaps against one of the teachers, would be very popular.

Lucy hurried off to find Tim's sister, Pokehead. Lucy was good at skipping and Pokehead (who, as Tim knew, also happened to be naturally good at throws, chokes and strangleholds) was her favourite skipping partner. Lucy was sure that a skipping demonstration would be very popular.

At home that night they talked about the talent show to Mum and Dad.

"Aren't you going to do something together?" Dad asked.

No one else, including Mum, thought this was a sensible idea.

It wasn't just that Will didn't know the words to 'Two Six Nine, The Goose Drank Wine', or that Lucy couldn't manage an effective flying armbar. It was that older brothers do not, ever, do talent shows with younger sisters. This was explained to Dad.

"Never?" he asked.

"Never," Will and Lucy said firmly, together.

Over the next few weeks, Will and Tim and Lucy and Pokehead practised and practised their acts until they were perfect, and then – four days before the talent show

– both Tim and
Pokehead came
down with flu.
There was a
lot of it about.

Will hurried round to all his other friends, but they were already doing acts of their own. It was the same with Lucy's friends.

"What are we going to do?" she said.

"It's a disaster," Will said, scowling. "Tim and I were certain to win, and now we can't even enter, and the worst thing is, it's not even anyone's fault."

He scowled so much he had a coughing fit, and Lucy asked if he was coming down with flu too, and Will said he might as well be, now that they couldn't enter the talent show.

They talked to Mum and Dad. Dad kept his mouth shut, but Mum wondered if Will and Lucy might think about doing an act together now – and, when they had stopped staring at her in disgust, she explained that it was the only way they could enter the talent show and win the prize. That made them think.

"But what would we do?" Will

said. "Lucy can't do much."

"Will can't skip," Lucy said. "He can't sing. He doesn't even know how to play the triangle."

After they had stopped arguing, Mum said, "What about magic?"

"But we don't know any," Will said.

"And who would teach us?" Lucy said.

Everyone was silent again, until Dad finally opened his mouth. "Uncle Joe?" he said, cautiously.

Mum looked at him sharply.

"Well, he does magic," Dad said.

"He's the most irresponsible man I know." Mum continued to look at Dad. "*One* of the most irresponsible men I know."

Will asked with interest, "Uncle Joe who set fire to himself?"

Lucy added, smiling, "Uncle Joe with the fancy suit?"

And they said, together:

"Good idea!"

One of the oddest things about the Quigleys was that, although Will was excitable and thoughtless, and Lucy was the smallest (and quietest), they often got their own way. Neither Mum nor Dad could explain this. But it was true.

Magic Uncle Joe

Uncle Joe lived on his own in a very messy flat which smelled of curry and aftershave. When Will and Lucy arrived, he wasn't wearing his fancy suit. He hadn't shaved either, and he must have forgotten about them coming because he seemed surprised to see them. But he was very friendly in an aimless sort of way, and he promised to teach them some magic.

"What are you after?" he asked. "Something simple, like this?"

He bent over Lucy and plucked a large gold medallion from behind her left ear.

"Or something a bit fancier, like this?"

He dropped the medallion into his trouser pocket, clapped twice, asked Will to check his own pockets – and there it was!

Uncle Joe had a big, lazy smile. "I'm not really meant to show you how it all works," he said. "But hey."

Over the next two days, he showed Will and Lucy how to pull rabbits out of hats ...

how to turn walking sticks into bunches of flowers ...

how to make ping-pong balls appear in people's mouths, and lots of other surprising things.

Will and Lucy got more and more excited.

"We're going to win this talent show for sure," Will said to Lucy. "Let's do the trick with the disappearing money. I'm sure one of the teachers will lend us some."

But Lucy wanted to do the trick where the playing cards turned into goldfish.

They couldn't agree. They kept arguing. Will had another coughing fit.

"You argue a lot, don't you?" Uncle Joe said. He wasn't used to children and was beginning to look tired.

"Have you got any more tricks to show us, Uncle Joe?" Lucy asked.

"No. Well, only one. But it's a bit dangerous."

"Show us, Uncle Joe."

"I really don't think I should."

"Please, Uncle Joe."

"Well, do you promise not to argue over it?"

They promised.

"All right then," he said.

It was the sawing-someone-in-half trick. Uncle Joe showed them the box where someone lies down with their head sticking out of one end and their feet sticking

out of the other. And he showed them the sword, which slices through the middle of the box.

"It's a bit razor-sharp," he said, looking doubtful.

"I already have a Swiss Army knife," Will said. "Which I'm allowed," he added.

Uncle Joe thought about this. "It's actually not a hard trick," he explained. "And it's always the most popular trick in the show. You just have to be a bit careful, because of the, um, razor-sharp sword."

"Don't worry, Uncle Joe," Lucy said. "You're no more irresponsible than Dad. Mum said."

Uncle Joe brightened. "Okay, then," he said. "I'll show you how it works, and, if you like it, you can borrow the stuff."

The Great Quiglondo

On the night of the talent show everyone was very excited. Except the teachers. The lighting system was playing up. Mr Sheringham was in his usual wet-faced panic and the head-teacher, Miss Strickland, strode in and out of the hall, whirring to herself and looking stern.

At seven o'clock Mum and Dad joined the crowd going into the school and took their places near the back of the hall. They were in a good mood. For the last few days, Will and Lucy had got on surprisingly well together.

"That trip to Uncle Joe's seems to have done them good," Dad said.

"Yes. I'm just a bit worried about Will's health. He keeps coughing, and this morning he looked as if he were running a temperature."

"He'll get through it, I'm sure."

"By the way," Mum said. "What magic trick are they doing?"

"I don't know. I thought you knew. They said they'd told you."

"I've no idea. They said you were going to talk to them about it."

They thought about this. Dad looked vague. "I'm sure it'll be fine," he said. "Joe's not much of a magician. It'll be something pretty tame, I expect."

The show began.

There were a great many different acts, including three other magicians. None was very good. The best was a sad-faced boy calling himself Magic Max, who lobbed eggs into an impossibly small glass of water on the other side of the stage. He solemnly smashed a dozen eggs against the far wall, and burst into tears.

Backstage, Will and Lucy waited to come on. Will was wearing a black cape with the words 'The Great Quiglondo' stuck to the back with sticky tape, and Lucy was dressed as a bee. There was no need for her to be a bee, but it was her favourite costume.

They sat backstage next to their box, which Uncle Joe had delivered to the school that morning, and which had attracted a lot of admiring attention from the other performers.

There was only one problem. Will was feeling ill.

For several days his throat had been sore and his nose blocked, and he couldn't stop coughing. Now he felt hot and sweaty, and he kept trembling. Worse, his mind kept wandering, which made him confused.

"Are you all right, Will?" Lucy asked.

"No. I'm not ill. I mean, yes," he said, in a low, distracted voice.

"Will you be okay with the razor-sharp sword?"

"Sword?" Will mumbled.

Then it was time for them to go on stage.

Uncle Joe had told them how to set up the box. It was quite easy. There were handles for lifting up the top, so that Lucy could climb in, and a slot for the sword to slice into, to cut her in half.

There was a handle on the side so that Will could pull the two halves of the box apart, and show everyone that Lucy was properly sliced in two.

On the back of the box there was a button which set off a lighting and smoke display, but this didn't work properly, and Uncle Joe had made Will promise not to touch it.

The audience became very excited when they saw the box. A rumour went round that The Great Quiglondo was going to cut the bee in half.

"What's everyone saying?" Dad asked. "And what's that box for, do you think?"

Mum went pale. "I'm starting to have bad feelings about this," she said.

In the wings, Mr Sheringham could be seen nervously consulting his list of acts.

Then silence fell as The Great Quiglondo began his patter – something about the ancient art of human sacrifice – but it was hard to make out, because he was mumbling and getting mixed up.

"And with this bee I'll slice in two my lovely sword," he burbled.

He attempted to lift up the top of the box and nearly fell over. He was sweating and his face was white.

"Will!" Lucy hissed.

"Not now," he mumbled back. "Have to lie down … Sleep …"

He climbed into the box, lay

down and shut the lid on top of himself.

The audience murmured, confused. For a moment, Lucy was afraid that everything was lost. But she was a determined girl and didn't like things being lost. She was a clever girl, too.

When Uncle Joe had explained how the trick worked, she had listened very carefully, and now she thought she could manage it herself, probably. So, before the audience could get too restless or Mr Sheringham could run onto the stage and stop everything, she said, in a sort of low, solemn squeak, "The Great Quiglondo is in his ancient box."

"This is the good bit," she added in her normal voice.

Remembering what Uncle Joe had said, Lucy used both hands to lift the sword off its cradle. It was heavier than she'd thought it would be.

"Razor-sharp," she said.

Someone in the audience laughed nervously.

"It is," Lucy said crossly. "Like a razor." She attempted to lift it up, to show everyone, but it was too heavy, and it swung sideways and sliced through one of the curtains at the side of the stage.

There were no more laughs.

There was a sort of frozen silence. Mr Sheringham was particularly frozen, especially his wet face.

"There," Lucy said. "Now I have to be very careful with the next bit because I haven't done it before. But if I can just get this sword up here," (grunting as she lifted it) "I can line it up here," (poking her tongue out as she concentrated very hard) "and then ram it into here …"

The razor-sharp sword fell into the slot with a meaty swish, plunging through the middle of the box, and Will groaned loudly and gave a great twitch.

At the back of the hall Mum and Dad leaped to their feet. In the wings, Mr Sheringham took a few rapid steps forward.

"Hang on a second," Lucy said. "Or I might do something wrong."

Everyone froze again.

"First," Lucy said, "I have to pull this." She pulled the handle on the side, and the two halves of the box shunted apart.

Will gave another groan as his head went one way and his wriggling toes went the other, and everyone else gave a groan as they saw that he was completely cut in half.

"And last," Lucy said, "I have to press this. I think."

She pressed the button that Uncle Joe had told Will not to press, and immediately there was a flare of light, a huge belch of smoke and a loud bang. All the stage-lights suddenly went out, and everyone got to their feet and began to shout.

The shouting stopped, just as suddenly, when the lights came on again. Mr Sheringham was crouching wetly by the fuse-box at the front of the stage, and Miss Strickland was standing and whirring above him. Lucy was in Mum's arms, and Dad was staring in horror into the box ... which was empty.

Throughout the hall there was total, horrified silence.

Then someone sneezed.

In the middle of the middle row, the sad-faced boy calling himself Magic Max leaped to his feet.

Sitting next to him, looking very woozy, was The Great Quiglondo.

Will looked up at Max blearily.

"What are you doing?" he said. "I haven't finished cutting you in half yet."

And he fell asleep again.

Joint Winners

Several days later, when Will had recovered, he and Lucy went up on stage again to receive their prize. There had been some doubt among the judges as to whether the trick had been the best thing they had ever seen, or the very worst. No one knew how it had been done, and Lucy hadn't told anyone, and Will had no idea. But in the end, for sheer entertainment, the prize was awarded jointly to The Great Quiglondo and the Bee.

"Jointly," said Dad, when they got it home. "I like that."

"It was mainly me," Lucy said.

"It wouldn't have been you at all if it hadn't been for me," Will said.

And, jointly, they began to argue.